The Seat Perilous

Arthur's Knights and the Ladies of the Lake

June Peters & Bernard Kelly

Series Originator: Fiona Collins

The History Press

For Stefan

First published 2013

The History Press
The Mill, Brimscombe Port
Stroud, Gloucestershire, GL5 2QG
www.thehistorypress.co.uk

British Library Cataloguing in Publication Data.
A catalogue record for this book is available from the British Library.

ISBN 978 0 7524 8970 4

Typesetting and origination by The History Press
Printed in Great Britain
Manufacturing managed by Jellyfish Solutions Ltd

Ancient Legends Retold: An Introduction to the Series

This book represents a new and exciting collaboration between publishers and storytellers. It is part of a series in which each book contains an ancient legend, reworked for the page by a storyteller who has lived with and told the story for a long time.

Storytelling is the art of sharing spoken versions of traditional tales. Today's storytellers are the carriers of a rich oral culture, which is flourishing across Britain in storytelling clubs, theatres, cafés, bars and meeting places, both indoors and out. These storytellers, members of the storytelling revival, draw on books of traditional tales for much of their repertoire.

The partnership between The History Press and professional storytellers is introducing a new and important dimension to the storytelling revival. Some of the best contemporary storytellers are creating definitive versions of the tales they love for this series. In this way, stories first found on the page, but shaped 'on the wind' of a storyteller's breath, are once more appearing in written form, imbued with new life and energy.

My thanks go first to Nicola Guy, a commissioning editor at The History Press, who has championed the series, and secondly to my friends and fellow storytellers, who have dared to be part of something new.

Fiona Collins, Series Originator, 2013

Acknowledgements

O ur first thanks are to our writing partner, Stefan Reekie, who has been the great guiding ear behind this book. We would also like to thank Fiona Collins who had the vision to create the series and Nicola Guy who had the courage to commission it. Both have provided patient, kind encouragement throughout.

We are also grateful to Ashley Ramsden and Tony Aylwin whose work has enriched many aspects of this book.

In 1992 Ashley led a workshop with Bernard called the Seat Perilous where some of the material presented here was explored for the first time.

We both worked with Tony on some of his pioneering Arthurian group performances and if you are a looking for a model for our King Arthur, you need look no further than him.

We would also like to acknowledge Sue Drainey and Anne Worthington for providing insights into the inner meanings of these stories, and Jamie Crawford and Sue Hollingsworth, both of whose work broadened our understanding of the material.

A special thanks to Michelle Hawkins for creating space so that the book could be completed, and to Ruby and Oscar Kelly-Hawkins for helping to shape the stories we tell. Finally our thanks go to Bob Peters for his endless support and kind advice.

Introduction

The Seat Perilous or Siege Perilous is the vacant chair that sits at the round table in King Arthur's court. This mysterious piece of furniture has been part of Arthurian literature for nearly one thousand years.

This literature is a complex cat's-cradle of interweaving narratives which often contradict themselves and each other. These narratives and the characters they contain continue to grow and evolve.

Over the centuries, specific characters and themes are foregrounded in importance and then fade. For instance, Sir Lanval was internationally known in the twelfth century as a knight who was generous to a fault. He's seldom heard of today, while Arthur, Merlin and Guinevere can be seen weekly on television in forms that those of the twelfth century might not recognise. Similarly the Grail, which is intimately connected with the Seat Perilous, changes its name, qualities, function and nature over time. It's sometimes a serving bowl, a basin, a chalice or a stone. It is always a mysterious object with Christian symbolism – but the associations and levels of specificity change: it's a source of healing; it can only be seen by one who is worthy; it's a cornucopia of plenty which will satisfy all needs; it sustains life; it was the vessel which caught the blood of the crucified Christ.

In the same way, the origin and what the seat signifies is also in flux. The Seat

Perilous recalls the chair left empty at the table of Joseph of Arimathea, which in turn resonates with Christ's seat at the last supper, or the empty place that Judas left behind; some say Uther Pendragon, the father of King Arthur, created the seat at the command of Merlin; others that Merlin himself made it and brought it fully formed to the table. Meanings are always crowding in, shouldering forward, and shoving others out of the way.

A constant quality of the seat, in most of the literature, is that only the most worthy knight can sit in it. Those who are unworthy are consumed by fire. One tale tells of a French knight, Sir Brumant l'Orguilleus, who once made a boastful vow that he was destined to sit there and then realised his mistake – but it was too late by then. He wept all the way to Arthur's court, sat on the seat and burst into flames. Your word really was your bond in those days.

There is always a potential most worthy knight. But the name and nature of that man also varies. In earlier versions, Sir Percival takes up that place. When he sits in the seat, he restores to life all those who were destroyed by it. Then the title of most worthy knight shifts to Sir Galahad, then back again to Sir Percival under the guise of Parzifal with a little help from Wolfram von Eschenbach and Wagner. And with this subsequent sidelining of Galahad, great stories, like the story of his birth have also dropped out of popularity.

Given this wealth and tangle of material, our job as storytellers is to listen to which manifestation of the characters, events and narratives speaks loudest to us, and then to see how we can tell that tale to best serve the times we live in.

As well as wishing to spotlight the stories of some of the lesser-known knights, we found ourselves drawn to two particular themes. The first is the journey of a knight

from youth to maturity and his relationship
with the ladies he meets on the way:

> The knight errant wanders in a potentially lim-
> itless divagation between beginning and end,
> which is also a realm of potential error, delu-
> sion, lostness, enchantment ... watched over
> by a lady who is often a figure of mediation.
> This forest is also the space of the inherited or
> appropriated remainders of Celtic myth which
> delineated a terrain imbued with marvels and
> to some extent free from morality, history and
> political reality.[1]

Secondly, we were interested in the theme
of the Ladies of the Lake as powerful pre-
Christian figures with their own agency. All
these extraordinary female characters in the
early stories are associated with rivers, pools
and wells. By bestowing sovereignty they
make things happen.

They are a fluid force which cannot be
controlled. They are dangerous and so

face danger. Ladies who "by virtue of their sex they should be protected, but by virtue of their sexuality they deserve to die".'[2]

Not surprisingly, by the end of Malory's *Morte D'Arthur*, most of these ladies are nuns. The stories of this shift in power mark a break – a pivotal moment in which belief changes. This turning point can be seen in the transformation of Elaine's spring into a boiling bath, her imprisonment in it and her rescue from it, and also in the self-sacrifice of Percival's sister.

The sacrifice through the feminine makes the Grail possible. These events parallel the wounding and the healing of the Grail king.

The work of Anne Wilson has been influential in the retellings of some of the stories. She identifies in Arthurian Romance a phenomenon that the storyteller and the shaman take for granted – that a function of the traditional wonder tale is to take the listener through a series of emotional positions designed to gain control over particular aspects of the problems of being human. She calls these Magical Plots, not in the sense that the stories are about magic, but in the sense that the stories themselves act in the way that magic itself tradition- ally acts – as ritual control. She suggests that the Arthurian stories were originally Magical Plots, taken by the early writers who put a 'rational gloss' on them, trying to make rational what was, by its function and nature, irrational. The way in which the two fit together – the old traditional Magical Plot and the twelfth to twenty-first century literary gloss, leads to 'interesting and strange effects'.[3]

We found ourselves implicated in this process, sometimes seemingly against our wills. In some retellings of the stories, we have followed the logic of a plot, and in some we have followed a character who was just determined to be heard.

When reading this book, we urge you not to be constrained by arbitary gender boundaries. Remember, men can be maidens, women can be warriors and we can all go on that journey following the river to its source.

June Peters and Bernard Kelly, 2013

References

1   *The Place of Women in the Marte Darthur* by Elizabeth Edwards in *A companion to Malory* edited by Elizabeth Archibald, 1996
2   *Sir Thomas Malory* by Felicity Riddy, 1987
3   *Plots and Powers* by Anne Wilson, 2001

'While the road is the way of the knight and the river is the way of the lady, the most blessed places are the bridges where both meet.'

One

The Knight
without a Sword

It was Pentecost, the feast of tongues, and all the King's men had gathered at the Round Table. No knight was absent; no seat was empty, except the one that was always empty.

This was the time to talk; mostly of ladies, up towers and down wells; tales of ladies being rescued and sometimes tales of ladies doing the rescuing. It was a brave knight who told that kind of story.

There was a great appetite for this; to speak of what they had been doing when they were apart; a hunger to remember, to put the table back together again. And as the tales grew larger, so, it seemed, did the knights telling them.

And Authur, sitting next to his Queen, Guinevere, all the while, was watching and enjoying the world he had created.

It might never have ended had not a young lad rushed into the hall, waving his arms wildly. What he was saying could not be heard above the sound of the boasting, the toasting and the all-round good-natured banter.

Arthur raised his hand and all fell silent. But the wild animation of the boy continued, still screaming to be heard above a noise which was no longer there. He stopped, embarrassed, and then could not contain himself again.

'A marvel! Your Majesty! A marvel!'

'What kind of marvel?' asked Arthur, his face already lighting up.

'Out on the river, sire, a great stone floats over the water and out of it there sticks a sword.'

'A sword? A stone? That is my kind of marvel,' said the King, 'or at least it used to be.'

In truth it was everyone's kind of marvel and the knights who had not yet told their tales left their ladies still stuck in their towers and rushed out of the door with the others to see it for themselves.

The lad did not lie. There, by the water's edge, hovering in the air, was a sword in a stone. As they approached they saw inscribed upon its blade, the words, 'There shall never be a man who can hold me except one – a knight without fault.'

'Great sport,' cried Arthur 'Who will be the first to try?' No one moved. 'Sir Lancelot! Do not be so modest. Be the first and surely the last to take the challenge.'

A look passed between Lancelot and Guinevere which the King did not see. 'My lord, choose a better knight than me,' replied Lancelot.

'A better knight?' repeated Arthur. 'You are renowned as the best knight in the world!'

'Sometimes a reputation is bigger than the man who wears it,' said Lancelot, looking away.

'Well then, my nephew! Sir Gawain, you will surely try?'

'If the best knight in the world declines, then I, myself, a much lesser knight, will not try.'

'I command you,' said Arthur, now losing patience. So Gawain did try but the sword stayed firmly in the stone.

Sir Percival then stepped up, 'I will keep Sir Gawain company. A humiliation shared is surely a humiliation halved.' The sword did not move an inch.

At that moment a very large, florid-looking lady arrived on a very small white pony.

The lady was weeping and wailing. 'Where is he?' she demanded.

'Where is who?' asked Arthur.

'My beloved Sir Lancelot,' she sobbed.

'Madam, he is over there,' said the King, pointing to the knight. She climbed off her pony, marched right up to him and extravagantly wiped a tear away from a rather bloodshot eye.

'My dear Sir Lancelot, have you heard that soon you will no longer be the greatest knight in the world?' She emphasised the phrase 'no longer' loudly to the crowd.

He mumbled, 'Lady, I never thought I was. I urge you, please don't concern yourself.'

'But I am concerned,' she cried. 'The whole world is concerned. You are Arthur's best knight and the Queen's favourite. We all had such high hopes of you and now those hopes are dashed. Goodness knows we've all had so much to put up with these last years, what with the land withering and wasting, and that poor Grail king with his embarrassing wound.'

Arthur was trying to encourage others to take up the challenge of the sword, but everyone was now much more interested in what the lady had to say. She was telling Lancelot how he would never sit in the seat; how he was now second best; how upset Queen Guinevere would be; on and on she went.

Each time Lancelot tried to escape her, she would be off again with more weeping and wailing, and he would have been standing there still if a disappointed Arthur had not headed back towards the hall, and ordered everyone inside again.

But no sooner were they seated once more than there was a tumult of clattering as all the screens on the windows slammed shut. In that sudden half darkness the knights could just make out two figures moving slowly around the table. As their eyes adjusted to the lack of light, they could see that one was an old man and the other a young knight in red armour, without sword or shield.

The old man bowed towards the King. 'Mighty King, a greeting to you. Rejoice! Today I bring you the greatest knight in all the world. Today I bring you all your heart's desire; the one who will mend what's shattered, find what's lost; the one who will bring the wastelands back to life.' And he led the young Red Knight straight to the empty seat beside Sir Lancelot. 'Here,' he said, 'Sit in this seat that has been standing empty all these years waiting for you to come.'

'Wait,' said Arthur. 'That is the Seat Perilous. Only the best of knights can sit there. All lesser men who tried have been consumed by fire. I have seen many a man destroyed in that place. Be sure that you're the one.' Without hesitation the young Knight took up his place and the circle of the round table was complete at last.

There was a long silence as all eyes rested upon the youth and the knight who sat next to him. Everyone could see they were alike.

Then Sir Lancelot stood and said, 'Welcome my son, Galahad, to the brotherhood of this great table.' The King and his knights all rose and bowed to Galahad.

Arthur reached for his scabbard. 'I see you have no sword. Take mine.'

'I hear there is another one nearby,' replied Galahad. Arthur's eyes sparkled at the very thought. This was his kind of knight.

Now they were following Galahad out to the sword in the stone over the water. And in no time he was holding it above his head saying, 'This is the great sword of Balin, who claimed it before his time had come. I claim it for our time and with it will heal the King and restore the wastelands. Tomorrow the quest for the Grail begins.'

Sir Lancelot said that he would join his son on the quest. And all the other knights vowed as one to follow them.

The women were already grieving for their husbands, sons, brothers and lovers, for they knew not all who set out would return from such a quest.

The men concentrated on practical matters. Galahad still had no shield. Many knights offered him theirs. He declined each act of generosity gently. 'You will need it to protect your heart,' they said. He just laughed.

When the time came, Arthur rode with his men to the edge of the forest. And there he embraced each and every one. He watched as they went their separate ways, knowing that now the circle was broken it would never be made whole again.

Galahad set out with Sir Bors and Sir Percival and they rode together until they reached the crossroads. There the three agreed to part.

Bors said, 'I'll go east. I met a maid there once. She put a crown of flowers on my head. I didn't like it at the time.

Now I wonder if it rather suited me. I go to look for her again.'

Percival said, 'I've always sought my sister's blessing. She likes the sea and that is westerly so I'll follow that path.'

Galahad bade them both farewell and made his way south, riding up a river valley until he came to a spring bubbling up out of the earth, and beside it a stone chapel stood. He looked inside and saw a candle burning brightly, and in its light there sat a lady. He entered and she welcomed him.

'You've come at last,' she said.

'I cannot stay. I have a long journey in front of me.'

She smiled and said, 'Some journeys are made on foot, others on horseback and some take place between the lips of the one who speaks and the ears of the one who listens.'

'Then,' he said, 'tell me where I am headed and where I have come from.'

In the flickering light, her face seemed to change like the moon. One moment, she was as old as time. The next, fresh and wide-eyed, like one new born.

'Yes. I'll tell you tales of the early days long before you were born,' she said. 'Are you ready? It will take a while.' He settled down to listen in the candlelight.

Two

The Story of the Knight of the River

There was once a lad named Lanfal. He came to Arthur's court with money enough to support himself, his servants and his horse. The King welcomed him warmly, 'I knew your father well, and I miss him. But now you are here, his spit in image and, I'm sure, in courage and plain speaking.

Now sit amongst the young bucks at first, friend. They'll show you round, take you to practise and play on the meadows, and then when you've settled in, the older ones will advise you.'

Everyone welcomed him and the young knights whispered, 'You've come at the right time! This very evening is the Queen's feast! The May Feast! It's the best of all the festivals. Summer's coming. You're fortunate.'

Sir Lanfal laughed. 'I must speak the truth. I love a feast!' He was excited, ready to join in all the life of the court, ready to put all his skill, enthusiasm and strength into jousting and questing and some proper fighting. But in the turmoil of all that was new that afternoon, he lost sight of his young companions. At last he saw a big group of knights walking into the great hall and he joined them. There was a turbulent strength pulsing through him as he followed the throng in through the doors. He was hungry and looking forward to the eating, the drinking, the slaps on the back, the horseplay, the rough and the tumble. But it wasn't like that at all when he entered the hall.

Inside, it was very dark. Someone was singing very softly. He felt the closeness of the knights who walked before him and alongside him, and if they hadn't been there, he would have been lost, stumbling in the dark. The knights all started to sing but Lanfal didn't know the song.

At the centre of the hall, a single candle burned upon a table. The table was raised above them all, on a dais. Beside the candle gleamed a large bronze bowl. Lanfal stopped, and let the knights walk past him, singing softly as they went.

Then the song stopped and for the first time he saw Queen Guinevere.

She was standing on the dais. How did she get there? She wasn't there when he walked into the hall! What was a woman doing here? Where was all the fighting?

The horseplay? Why was everyone so old? Where were the other lads he'd met that day?

The Queen held the bronze bowl. The candle flickered, but all the light seemed to come from her. She gazed into the bowl, and began to speak. 'Who commands the tides to ebb and flow? Who calls the water in the wells to rise and fall? Who brings the rains that feed the land' Then she tipped the bowl. A stream of water poured out. It shimmered golden in the light, then seemed to disappear into the air.

The men were singing again, very softly. All except Lanfal, who, in the shadows, stood mouthing words he did not know. Then Arthur looked up at Guinevere and called out, 'All life comes from you. All power is bestowed by you. No greater light, no greater gifts. There is no lady as beautiful as you.' And all the knights repeated his words. Then the King cried out, 'Who do we serve?'

They all shouted, 'The Queen! The Queen! The Queen!'

But Lanfal stood silent and bewildered. He spoke not a word.

The big doors were opening behind him now. And for one moment the Queen looked straight at the young knight. There seemed to be a question in her eyes. 'Are you ready?' 'Will you come?' And then they seemed to say, 'Last chance.' And his heart sang out 'You're beautiful.' But that seemed neither a manly nor a clever thing to say and the moment passed and she was gone.

Then the doors on the far side of the hall were thrown open and for an instant he was blinded by the light. There were the tables! There was the food and drink and bluster and loud laughter! The feast was beginning.

But now he felt cut off; that a distance had grown between him and the others. The new friends he thought he had made seemed to fall away. If someone called him to their side or welcomed him he did not hear it.

It was the same every day after that. He was as courteous as he knew how, as generous, as helpful, friendly and plain speaking as his father had taught him to be. But never from the moment that he left the darkness of the hall at the May ceremony did he see warmth or a sign of friendship. At this richest of courts, he saw that Arthur gave gifts to everyone else, but he never got a gift or the chance of advancement. No one seemed to notice his bravery or his skill.

At last he had spent the wealth he had brought with him. His servants left. He had to sell his saddle and then he had to sell the horse as well. What good was a knight without a horse?

Then one day he left the castle and wandered dejected and alone and lay down by the side of a stream. There he fell asleep and was woken by a tickle and wetness on his face. When he opened an eye, he was looking into a pair of huge flaring nostrils. A voice said, 'Here's a horse for you.' The nostrils receded and snorted and Lanfal sat up with a shock. There was indeed a horse. There was a young girl too, with a crown of flowers on her head. She smiled and said, 'Take him.'

Lanfal jumped to his feet. 'It's true I do lack a horse. But I must speak plain. I have no money to pay for it.'

'This horse is a gift from my mistress. He will be friend and companion and adviser to you. Let the horse read the road. Let him have his head. He'll take you along the right way.' And she handed him the reins.

Then she stroked the horse's nose as Lanfal climbed into saddle. The horse nuzzled the girl's hand, snorted again, turned and, leaving her behind, trotted up the road beside the stream with Lanfal on his back.

It was the horse who chose which track to take and all the way Lanfal did not complain. He let the horse have its head. And so he rode until the light that shone through the leaves told Lanfal that the sun was high above the forest. He heard the sound of a woman's voice singing. The horse stopped there and would not move on, but instead lowered his head and cropped the grass. Lanfal slid off the saddle and climbed the rocks beside the stream. He parted the bushes and looked through the branches. There was a pool, and in the pool there was a lady bathing. He felt his heart pound as if he was racing towards her. He had never seen a woman like this before.

He saw her cloak upon a tree and he reached up and lifted it lightly from the branch and went to the place at the pool where the water ran in. The lady turned and looked straight up at him from the pool. He tried to recall where he had seen that direct gaze before. Where he had felt like this before. He clutched the cloak and blushed. 'There is no greater beauty than yours.' And she smiled.

She stepped out of the pool and said, 'Give me my cloak' He stepped forward and wrapped it around her.

Beside the pool was fruit and bread and drink. Lanfal and the lady sat together there. She said, 'Now is the time to speak.'

He said, 'I am a knight in the court of Arthur. I do the best I can. I am loyal and true. But my King bestows no rank or duties on me and I am part of the court, but not part of the company.'

She nodded. 'You made a bad start. The King is a good king and you do right to show him loyalty. But in the presence of the Queen, you were silent when you should have spoken. You were a bewildered boy.'

He began to protest at the description but she just smiled again and at the curve of her lips, he felt himself unmasked and he began to laugh. 'And here I am a man at last?'

'Not just that,' she said. 'You are soon to be a true knight of the world,' and then she kissed him.

When the time came for him to return to Arthur's court, she said, 'Hold me in mind.'

'That won't be hard,' he replied.

'When you call me, I will be there,' she promised. 'But watch that plain tongue of yours. Don't speak my name or talk about me to anyone. Keep me in your heart and not on your lips for bragging.' And Lanfal promised he would.

Then Lanfal found himself on the road again, once more mounted on his wise horse, and he made his way back to the castle and Arthur's court. As he passed through the gates of Camelot, this time the knights, young and old, all greeted him as if he were a brother returned from the dead. Everywhere people seemed glad to see him.

That evening as he entered the hall, the King embraced him and said, 'Lanfal! Welcome! Come and sit by me. I haven't had your company for a long while. How is it I haven't seen you? Tell me of your adventures.' The only adventure Lanfal could think of was the adventure with the lady but he kept quiet about that and instead told a tale of his father's valour and claimed it for himself. And when he'd finished the King said, 'I enjoyed your tale.' Then he placed his hand upon his shoulder, 'And I see there is another story in your eyes. You're wise to keep it close. But one day we'll get it out of you.'

That night, when Lanfal stepped into the darkness of his chamber, he locked the door, bowed his head and he called her name. And there she was. She sat with him. He talked. She listened, advised him and stayed until first light. Then she was gone.

The next day Lanfal received a gift from the King – a fine saddle and a bag of gold. A few days later, he offered him a seat in the circle at the table. And there were jousts and work to do to serve his King.

The lady of the pool was always in his mind and in his heart, but only when he was alone did he speak her name, whispered on a breath, and in that moment she was with him again.

And as the court year turned through all its phases and its festivals, so Lanfal prospered. At the autumn equinox he was the coming man. At winter solstice he was influential and by the time the May festival had come round again, he was a favoured knight with all that this entailed.

As he approached the hall this time, he had many friends calling, 'Lanfal! Here! Here! Come walk with me!' They walked together into the dark hall. They were joining in, singing softly. Now he knew the words.

In the centre of the hall, there was the single candle and the bronze bowl. He stood not at the back, but in plain view at the front. But still he did not see the moment she arrived. She was just there, in the light, holding the bowl, with the golden waters reflected on her face.

He saw the stream of shimmering water fall and disappear into the air. He heard the singing, saw Arthur raise his hand and heard his voice, gentle and deep, 'All life comes from you. All power is bestowed by you. No greater light, no greater gifts. There is no lady as beautiful as you.' And all the knights repeated his words.

Lanfal heard the words and opened his mouth to speak, but suddenly before his eyes was a vision of his lovely lady of the pool. Arthur called, 'Who do we serve?'

All the knights responded, 'The Queen! The Queen! The Queen!'

All except Lanfal, who did not speak.

When he had been a lad in the shadows at the back of the crowd, no one had noticed him. But this time he had a place of rank. Guinevere saw his silence. She looked straight at him. She said nothing, but Arthur followed her gaze and said, 'Lanfal, speak.'

Lanfal just stared ahead. 'I cannot,' he said.

The knights on either side of him whispered, 'You must speak, Lanval! Or you do disservice to our lady.'

'If I speak, I must speak plain.' And to the whole assembly he said, 'Our Queen is beautiful, but I know a lady as lovely and as bright.' He never was a man to whisper.

The doors to the hall flew open and a great wind blew the candle out. Guinevere was gone and all the men were scattering and the voices of the many were crying 'Disrespect,' 'Sin,' 'Treachery' and in the darkness Lanfal felt hands seize him – and there was confusion. Some were calling for him to be punished there and then. Some were buffeting him. He was dragged out into the evening light.

'Hang him!' they cried.

But Lancelot was striding to the front of the crowd, 'He's young. Don't do this. The Queen has her own ways to deal.'

Sir Owain said, 'There should be one to counsel him.'

And the King cried out, 'Lanfal. You say you know one as lovely. If you can show us such a lady, I'll free you from this threat of death.'

In the chapel, Galahad looked up as the lady gave a sigh. 'Poor young man, who did his growing up to manhood all back-wards and in public!

Who knows if beauty is the source of love or love the source of beauty? Is it a quality of the beloved or of the lover's gaze? Who cares! His lady doesn't. Nor the Queen.'

They took him to his chamber and there, alone, he called out her name. She was in his mind, his heart. He looked to the shadowy corner where she used to come. But there was no sweet word, no soft touch. He called again. She did not come.

There was nothing to do but to return to the courtyard where a scaffold was already standing and Arthur on his seat before it. Lanfal bowed. He said, 'I cannot show her, even though I hold her in my heart.' And, looking upwards, he saw, framed in a window high above, that Guinevere was watching. He said again, 'I hold her in my heart!'

As he climbed the scaffold steps, his face was shining. One knight said, 'He looks as if he's going to a wedding, not a hanging.'

Another shouted, 'He's clearly gone mad.'

But Lancelot said, 'The lad's in love and who's to say his is a lesser love than the one that we have for our Queen?'

As Lanfal reached the top, the hangman stepped towards him, swinging the gallows rope in his hands. Then at that very moment a horn sounded from outside the walls, and there was a clatter of hooves, as into the courtyard came a woman richly dressed, riding on horseback. It was his lady. She raised her eyes to Guinevere at the window and bowed her head. And

Guinevere returned the greeting and smiled, 'A welcome to you, sister.' No other word was spoken by anyone. No more needed to be said. The proof was before all eyes that here were ladies, equal in beauty and power; sisters, and queens both.

And as suddenly as she had come the lady turned her horse and was cantering off through the gates, and she had spared not one glance for Lanfal.

And with her departure, Guinevere gave a sign to dismiss the hangman and was gone from the window. Everyone started talking at once.

Lanfal leapt from the scaffold and ran towards his horse, scrambled into the saddle and he and the horse were away and out of the gates, after his lady. He rode hard at a gallop to catch her up. But the lady was always far ahead – just visible in the distance, riding with ease, at a gentle trot. At last he saw that she was approaching a river whose waters were wild and deep and white with foam. He called out her name. And at these words, she stopped.

He found that he was close beside her. Above the roar of the river, her voice was clear and distinct. 'Come no further.' She said. 'Do not speak my name again. You have betrayed me.'

'How is it betrayal to love you and hold you dear and speak only of your beauty and your worth?' he asked.

'On May Feast last that's when you should have spoken of beauty, but you were silent. Now at this May Feast you have spoken, when you should have kept your peace. In making comparison, you have diminished us both. Give to each lady what belongs to each lady. Return to Arthur's court and give your Queen her due.'

'You are my Queen,' he cried. 'And if you cross the river I will come after you and follow you till the end.'

She gave no answer, but turned to the rushing waters, reached out her hand and the river became shallow and slow, and her horse waded easily across. Lanfal watched her till her horse was clambering up and onto the far bank and then he made to follow her into the shallows, but as he did the waters of the river were once more a grey and thundering maelstrom. He pulled his horse back quickly, but then he shouted, 'Even so, I take the adventure. I will follow you till I die.'

She turned then and saw Lanfal and his horse together plunge into the wild river. The horse was swimming strong through the torrent. But the power of the current was stronger still and Lanfal felt his grip slip and he slid from the horse's back into the swirling waters below.

The water swallowed him, released him and then dragged him under once again. He sank and rose and sank and rose until the power of the deluge was sweeping him away. She saw the choice he had made, held out her hand and, as she did, the river calmed and carried him to the bank below her, where the rocks and reeds and water weeds caught him and held him fast. The lady stepped down onto the rocks to the place where the waters eddied round him. She reached down and pulled him to safety.

She took the cloak from her own shoulders and wrapped its warmth around his wet body. And then she helped him up onto her horse and rode with him away from Arthur's realm.

Knights who went riding deep into the forest came back with stories of how they had seen the horse, still saddled, but running wild. No one could catch him.

'Did Lanfal never return?' asked Galahad.

'On just one evening of the year – the Queen's May Feast, Pentecost, we call it now – the horse has a rider on its back. Beside them, there's a lady, mounted, dressed in silks of blue and green.

Together they ride along the river path.

The rider guards the lady. The lady guards the river.

Her gaze is on the waters. She commands them to rise and fall.

His gaze is on the lady. He keeps his silence now.'

Three

The Tale of the Knight with Two Swords

Balin and Balan were brothers. They were young. Balan was the older, but there was not a year between them and they were like twins in appearance and nature and they loved each other dearly.

They both possessed the knightly virtues of honesty, bravery, bulky blonde good looks and the willingness to take the head off any stranger who challenged them, contradicted them or stood in their way. Sometimes just a sideways look would start the fight.

The regime of the court brought a change in Balan. He became more thoughtful and more disciplined. Balin became, if anything, more boisterous and reckless. He sought out company – not always the best – and company sought him out too. He was passionate, wild and impetuous. He acted before thinking and would swing his sword before asking any question or giving any reason. If his heart said 'Do it' then he did it. Then it was usually brother Balan's job to talk him out of trouble.

But one day Balin went too far. There was a brawl. It began as a fist fight between two lads – Balin and a young cousin of the King. But Balin was large and he didn't know his strength and he killed Arthur's kinsman with a single blow. Even his brother's articulate defence could not soften the pain in the King's heart and Balin was locked up in the dungeons to give him time to consider his actions. For many long days and nights Balin lay in the dark on a bed of straw with just a little water to drink and a little bread to eat and only a very little light to see by. The gaoler said, 'Why are you complaining lad? You're noble born so you get the clean straw and water. Would you rather I swap it for the fetid straw and the stinking water I give to the common prisoners?'

Then one day it wasn't the gaoler's silhouette there in the doorway, or his rough and ready greeting. It was that familiar beloved voice saying, 'Brother, you are free to go. Come. I've brought food and wine,' and they walked out into the clean air. They sat together under the evening sky and ate the bread and drank wine and kept company. Till Balan said,

'Now listen. It was hard work to get you out of a fix this time. Little brother, it's time to grow up. The King commands I must ride out on my quest. I have to be obedient and to leave you. I won't be here to get you out of trouble next time. You must go to our King and bow and ask forgiveness, and learn to be patient. I have given the gaoler money for new clothes and he's to give you a good wash and a shave, and sweeten you and bring you your horse. Goodbye. I'll see you in the spring for the Queen's festival.' And he kissed him, and then he was off on his horse, trotting out of the gates with Balin running, laughing alongside, till he was left behind. Balin waved until his brother was gone from view. Then he spread his arms wide and leaped in the delight of being free. He returned and knocked on the gaoler's door, but there was no answer.

He knew he should wait. But he could clearly hear the roar of laughter and the clash of cups coming from Arthur's hall. It was so close! He knew he should wait. He knew he couldn't go. Of course he couldn't go as he was – all smelly in rags and tatters, all unkempt and unshaven, but while he was waiting for his bath and for his new clothes, he had to have a look and see what was going on. He had already forgotten his brother's wise words.

When he came to the gates of the hall, the guards recognised him. They knew of his reprieve. He exchanged a joke with them and, laughing, they nodded him through. He'd always been the most forgivable of rascals. Balin slipped inside and hid behind a curtain near the door.

Through a gap, he could see the knights and their ladies at the tables set for supper. He could see Arthur and the Queen shining beside him and across the table, beside Sir Lanceclot, the empty place. The seat of dread! How he longed for himself to be the one – the best and the most fearless. The most noble! If only he had the chance to sit there he would brave the peril of it.

Suddenly the shouting and the laughter stopped and the uproar faded to quiet gasps. Then there was silence and Balin thought, 'They have smelled me and are disgusted.' His impulse was to rip aside the curtain and present himself as he was, ragged and dirty, and to cry out, 'Yes! I'm back. So take me as I am!' But then he heard the King's voice say, 'Lady!'

'Lady?' Clearly he wasn't the focus of attention after all. Somewhat disappointed, he put an eye again to the gap.

The feast was now a frozen tableau – wine cups held suspended in mid air, roast meat hovering before wide open mouths; all eyes fell on the lady who stood before them. She was simply clothed in a cloak of blue, standing in the full light away from the dark where Balin hid. As he watched, she swept back her cloak, reached for the clasp and let the cloak fall at her feet, and everyone gasped again. At her waist, the lady wore a sword belt and a scabbard and a sword within the sheath. Then Arthur stood and spoke, 'Lady your garments are fine, but the sword becomes you not.'

And the lady said, 'Well I know it. Yet I have no choice. It is a burden I must bear and cannot cast it off, but have to carry it till it's taken from me by another.'

And the King pushed away his dish and set his elbow on the table, and his forefinger and his thumb to his cheek and his chin, which everyone knew to mean, 'I love a story. No one will eat until I've heard this one!'

So, standing in the shadow of the doorway, Balin heard the tale the lady told.

'This is the sword of the one who will be best of all his generation. And I am under a cross and a spell, and knotted into my hair is the fate that I must carry this sword through the land until I find the knight who can relieve me of its weight.'

Arthur rose. He bowed his head and then they were face to face. He placed one hand on the scabbard at her hip, and the other on the pommel of the sword by her breast. Then he tugged. Then he pulled and he strained till his brow was wet. But none of his strength would shift the sword from the sheath. At last he stopped. 'Once I was well known for work like this – but it seems I already have my lady's sword and must be content with that. The better knight is yet to come.' He smiled, turned, and, hand on heart, he bowed to Guinevere who raised her eyes and returned his smile as if to say, 'Those were indeed great days.'

Then Gawain tried but the result was the same. Then all the knights of the round table tried. But there was no better ending for anyone.

And the lady sighed and said, 'Ah! I had thought that at the court of King Arthur I would find the knight who would lift this burden from me.'

And Balin was bursting with desire to try and prove himself. Any small reserve of self-restraint that he might have gained in prison was all used up and he could bear it no more. He jumped out from behind the curtain, big and broad and bulky, dressed in rags, and, dirty and unshaven as he was, he strode towards the lady thrusting out his hand.

The lady backed away. But the King stepped forward and, turning towards her, said, 'No, Madam. Don't turn away. This is Sir Balin – a hothead youth who killed my cousin in a brawl and now returns from imprisonment. This is a knight who has made mistakes but he's done his time, he's paid his price. He is a worthy knight. Forgiveness also has its seat in Arthur's hall. Give him his chance.'

He looked at the young knight and said, 'Sir Balin. It is time to begin again.'

So the lady offered him the hilt and Balin, now face to face with her, took it and with one easy movement and a hiss of metal, drew the sword from the scabbard and held it shining high above her head.

The hall erupted in clapping and roaring and hooting and stamping of feet, and when at last it all died down, the lady spoke. 'Balin, by this act you have shown that you are destined to be the best of your generation. I bow to you and your potential. All hail to you and to your future deeds. This sword is yours. But I see that you are very young and have a deal of learning ahead of you yet. So give me back the sword and I will be the guard of it for you until the time that you are grown to be a proper man.'

But Balin's eyes were on the glory of the sword he held. It glimmered strangely in the candlelight. It had possession of his heart and he whispered, 'No.'

She said, 'Give me back the sword.'

He, still looking at its glitter, said, 'No. I won it and I'll keep it.'

The lady looked at him. 'It will be a sad thing for you, if you do. I ask you again for your sake and not for mine. Return that sword into my keeping until the time comes when you know enough, when you are strong enough to understand the power it holds.

'Your destiny and this sword mark your path as the true knight's path. But even so, if you keep the power that you have unleashed today, then all your good will turn to bad, and all your helping turn to hindrance and all your healing turn to harm.' She stared long and hard. He shook his head.

'In the end the sword's power, taking it as you do, too soon, wielding it as you will, in ignorance, will destroy both you and the one you love.'

But he, still looking at its great beauty, cried, 'I take the adventure.'

Without another word the woman pulled her cloak about herself, and, with the empty scabbard at her waist, she left the hall.

And everyone agreed that that was enough excitement for one feast at Arthur's table.

But they'd hardly had time to reach for their knives and cups before another lady entered the hall. Her face was dark and angry as a thunder cloud. Her hands in fists, she strode before the King and Queen, she pointed a menacing finger at Balin. 'A mistake's been made. Now Arthur, make a choice. This knight has stolen his lady's power and has gone against his lady's will. She has unwisely and unwillingly granted him this sword and he will wield it disastrously.'

Balin stuck out his chest and said, 'I am the best of my generation.'

She sneered and laughed, 'Look at you! You have come before the King and Queen without restraint, without respect, without preparing yourself, without cleaning yourself or taking effort to make yourself worthy. You have the power to wield the sword. But you have it without the effort of the journey and the quest. It's true you have the muscle to hold it, and the heart to strike with it, but have you the discipline to take the reins that control and guide your own heart? Look at you. No, you do not!'

She turned again to Arthur. 'A dam has burst. The current that carries this lad flows too soon. You must cut off his power at the source! Arthur, in the name of your Queen, I call on you to hunt down the lady who has given him this power, and bring me back her head!'

But before anyone could move, Balin was running full pelt across the floor towards the lady. He had the great sword and he was roaring loud, 'If there is a head to be had, it is this head before me now,' and he swung the sword.

There was terrible confusion and chaos in the hall. Afterwards, no one could agree what happened next. Many said that they heard the sound as the sword sliced first through air, then flesh and bone. Some said her head was still in his hand when he was hounded out of the hall. Some said it fell on the floor with a thud and when the gaoler came running in, he put it in a sack. But some said there was no thud, no body and no head. She disappeared before he struck her.

At last the gaoler did the job he had been paid to do. He cleaned Balin up and gave him fresh clothes and a horse. It should have been the joyful task of washing away the remnants of old mistakes from a man who had made amends. But this new start was already stained with fresh blood. He was banished now from King Arthur's court.

The gaoler was the only one to bid Balin goodbye when he rode out, with two swords at his belt – the sword of his boyhood and the sword of the lady. 'I will win back my King's forgiveness and his love.' But even the gaoler knew that it was not the King whom Balin should be asking for forgiveness. He should be bowing down before the Queen.

Balin had an image of both his swords emblazoned on his shield so all would know him. At court in the years that followed, they heard many tales of the adventures of Sir Balin, the Knight with Two Swords. They heard how he got into arguments that weren't his own, how he swore his loyalty too soon and left a lot of dead and dying men and maidens in his track. They heard how hard he tried to win again the honour he had lost. He defeated Rince, the giant king. He fought knights and monsters, all to gain forgiveness from the King.

Arthur said, 'It's sad. His heart is good. He tries to do the right thing. He tries to help.'

Guinevere replied, 'He is like a river that has burst its banks. He is always in full flood. His power has no channel. He accepts no advice.'

Balin was very far from wise words now. For some time now he had been having a lot of trouble with an invisible knight. He'd bitten off more than he could chew and had put his enormous resources of strength, courage and good will towards protecting one who was almost immediately killed by the unseen knight. He had learned that Garlon was the name of the one who had shamed him so.

He swore to hunt this Garlon down and take his vengeance. He came at last to the Castle of Corbin and made himself congenial to the guards. 'You're very welcome, sir. But leave your weapons at the door,' said the gatekeeper. He left his lady's sword with them. But he kept the sword of his boyhood hidden under his cloak. And thus

he was welcomed with all trust by the King
of Corbin Castle.

When all sat down to dine, there was
another knight who suddenly appeared at
the table. He was big, young and unruly.
When Balin heard his name, 'Garlon,
cousin to the King', called across the table,
he knew that this was the enemy he sought.

Balin shouted out, 'You have slain
those under my protection and shamed
me!' In front of all, he seized his hidden
sword, leaped across the table, kicking
aside the goblets of wine and the good
bread, meat and fruit and, at a stroke,
Garlon was dead.

The King rose from his seat. 'The rules
of peace and brotherhood at my feast are
broken.' Then he called calmly for his
sword. You have shamed me. You bring
a sword to my table. You strike down my
kinsman who sat under my protection.'
Balin raised the sword of his boyhood to
defend himself, but with one sure stroke the

King broke it in two. Then Balin, a lad once more, was running for his life. He came to a place where two great oak doors opened easily and in that space there hung a shining spear. He grabbed it and turned. There was the King running towards him, his sword raised high. Balin threw the spear.

He always had a good aim.

The King dropped his sword and fell, clutching at the wound in his thigh and the blood that began to flow. Balin didn't see what happened after that. He remembered a rumble and a creak and the groan of stone. The castle was collapsing. His world was tumbling down.

Balin pulled the lady's sword out from beneath the rubble. Still he could not let it go. He rode on until at last he came to a very bright clear sign that read, 'Do not pass this sign.'

He rode past it.

He rode till he a came to a river and a jetty and a bright clear sign that said, 'Do not give up your shield.' He heard the suck and the slip of an oar in the water and a boat came into view. The boatman said, 'Oh master! Your horse is good, but where you must fight, that shield will be mighty flimsy. Rather you should give up that shield you hold and take this one. It's much stronger.' And really the shield the boatman held did look stronger. It wasn't Balin's shield and it didn't have the sign that showed all who he was, but it definitely looked stronger. And when he got out of the boat on the far side, he was carrying that shield.

He was in a strange land and seeking a fight. Beyond was a castle. It was the Castle of the Ladies. There was a knight standing guard at the drawbridge. The knight called out a challenge. Of course Balin could never refuse a challenge.

They fought together on the bridge, the strange knight and Balin with his new, unmarked shield. One moment he seemed like a man dancing with his own shadow; the next, like a murderer trying to destroy the darkness within himself. They were equally matched. Then each struck the other's death blow.

When the ladies of the castle saw both the knights fall, they went to tend them. The two lay side by side, like two lovers sleeping in each other's arms. The ladies sighed when they took off the knight's helmets. By their features, they knew them to be brothers. In the end Balin slew the one he loved, his brother Balan, and was slain by him. And so the prophecy of the lady of the sword was fulfilled.

'If only he had listened to me,' said the lady in the chapel, 'and given me back my sword. Then there would have been no wounded King, no wasteland and no need for you to carry it now.'

'You should always guard against being possessed by the things you desire', replied

Galahad. 'Yes,' said the lady, 'and this is as true for people as it is for swords.'

Four

The Tale of the Knight of the Well

S ir Owain was resourceful, strong and brave. But many questioned how it was that at his age he had never settled down and didn't seem to have a lady of his own to guide him. He was one of Arthur's favourites and the King held him in high regard.

One evening he and a small group of knights were sitting outside the King's chamber. The King was sleeping and the knights were waiting for him to rise so they all could go and eat supper. 'I'll tell you all a tale,' said Sir Calogrant. 'It's a story from long ago when I was young and arrogant.' He told his tale, and by the time he had finished it, Arthur was awake and they all went down to eat.

But Sir Owain could not forget the story he'd heard while Arthur slept. It was a strange one. It puzzled him.

There was a generous host who lived in a fine castle at the head of a river valley. There was a forest spirit who kept the wild creatures in their places. There was a lady with a secret well guarded by a Black Knight. You had to challenge the knight by splashing water from the well onto a stone. It was a good story, but it ended in a most unsatisfactory way. Sir Calogrant, the hero, was defeated. The Black Knight was the victor. The Black Knight took away Calogrant's horse. Calogrant was humiliated and had to be helped home by the generous host and nursed back to health.

The talk at supper was of the story. Arthur wanted to hear it too. Afterwards, Owain said, 'The ending's wrong. We can't leave our knight defeated. I am the man to put this right.'

'We all go forth to slay the world when we have drunk our fill,' sneered Sir Kay, the King's steward. 'But in the morning when we have sobered up, we find ourselves still safely in our beds.'

Sir Owain made his mind up there and then and, at first light, he slipped away. He rode till at last he came to a river, which he followed till it became a little stream. There, at the head of the valley, was a pleasant meadow and a fine castle, and two lads were playing at target practice on the grass.

They ran to get their father. He was the generous host Sir Owain had heard of in the story. He opened his arms wide and welcomed Owain in.

And there were the beautiful and gentle daughters of the host to tend to him and take him to supper. There he ate delicious food and was given every kind attention till his host said, 'Sir, what do you quest for?'

And he replied, 'I seek the Black Knight of the Well. Can you tell me the way?'

And his host said, 'You will find the Black Knight only with the help of the wild herdsman.'

'Where will I find the herdsman?'

'You will only find him when you have lost yourself in the forest.'

The next day, there was a sumptuous breakfast, and the beautiful daughters were again attentive, and then Sir Owain set off on his horse into the forest to get lost. Soon he had succeeded and could not tell one path from another, and that's when he heard the sound of the herdsman's horn. He saw the wind disturb the branches of the trees. They thrashed and parted and there, towering over him, was an extraordinary man. He was as tall as the trees themselves. He had only one eye and only one leg and the hair on his head was like the tangled forest undergrowth beneath him. Around his feet the forest creatures ran – the hare, the badger, the hedgehog and the fox. A stag walked by his side, its head held high, its massive antlers spreading. The giant's arms were as thick as the branches of the trees and in one hand he held a huge log as a club. Nestling in the tangle of his hair there was a small red squirrel looking out.

When he spoke his voice was the roar of the storm and his speech was rough, 'What are you doing here? This is the place of forest creatures. I am the one who appoints their place and keeps them safe. You are a creature of the castle. Return to your own place!'

But Owain called out that he sought the well, and when he heard this, the herdsman lifted up his club and brought it crashing down. It was as if the undergrowth was untangling itself. Owain saw that a path had appeared. He travelled along it till he came to a glade surrounded by leafy ash and oak. There was a well with an iron bowl joined to a chain and, next to it, a stone. He knew just what to do. He grasped the iron chain and lowered the bowl until he heard a splash. He pulled the bowl, now full of water, from the well and emptied it over the stone.

There was a flash of lightning and a deafening crack of thunder. The sky was suddenly black and a terrible storm broke over his head. Rain, wind and hail battered the trees where he and his horse sheltered.

Then the storm stopped as suddenly as it had begun. The glade was once more filled with sunlight. But every single leaf had been stripped from the trees. The branches were now filled with birds which all began to sing. As he listened to the beauty of the song, he heard another sound. It was the thud of horse's hooves and Owain readied himself for the challenge.

All the birds flew away as a huge black horse with a knight in black armour galloped into the glade. 'Who disturbs my lady's well?' he roared

There was a fight; a great clashing of swords. Then Owain cut through flesh to bone and his foe cried out for mercy but Owain had been planning the ending to this story for far too long to change it now. He killed the Black Knight there beside the well and waited, for he did not know what would happen next.

On a hill above the well, there was a tower. It was the tower of the Lady of the Well. In her tower, the lady felt the wind change and she knew that her knight was dead so she went out to meet the man who had killed him.

As she approached, Owain felt himself unsteady on his feet. Other than the Queen, he had never seen a woman as beautiful. He felt she had already taken his heart and had dropped it into the well and now it was falling into the depths below.

'You killed my knight,' she said. 'That makes you mine.'

'I would gladly be yours,' said Owain.

'To be my possession, to do with as I will?'

'I am yours to possess and yours to command,' said Owain

'Even to the point of death?' she asked

'Yes. To that point and beyond.'

'And if I command that you be killed for the murder of my lord?'

'Then I would fling my arms wide and run towards the point of your sword with a smile upon my face.'

'And why would you accept such punishment so willingly?' asked the lady.

'I am a prisoner of love,' said Owain.

'I see no gaoler. What holds you captive?' asked the Lady of the Well.

'My heart,' said Owain.

'What rules your heart?' asked the lady.

'Mine eyes,' said Owain.

'And what governs your eyes?' asked the lady.

'The dreadful beauty I see before me now,' said Owain.

'What is so dreadful about this?' she asked, raising her face towards the light.

'It is dreadful because I am lost within its gaze. It consumes me so you are all and I am nothing and if I knew it, I would cry out your name now, because I have forgotten my own.'

'And what am I to do?'

'Lady, you hold my heart hostage. Whether you eat it and spit it out or cradle it tenderly in your hands, it is yours forever now.'

Well, how could she refuse an offer like that?

So now Owain was the Black Knight of the Well who answered the thunder's call.

The years passed. Then one day he rode to the well all ready for a fight, only to find King Arthur there with a company of his knights.

Owain did not disclose his identity and when Sir Kay rode out to face the

Black Knight Owain made short work of him, but spared his life. The Black Knight then took off his helmet and Sir Kay staggered back. 'It's you,' he cried. 'Who do you serve?'

'I am lord, master and servant here,' said Owain. And for the first time that anyone could remember, Sir Kay was lost for words.

Then Arthur said, 'Here you are at last. You didn't tell us where you'd gone. We thought that you were dead. But here you are.'

All the knights that loved Owain, which were many, pleaded with him to return with them to Arthur's court. To each he said, 'My place is here with my lady.'

Then Gawain came to him and said, 'Do not become the kind of man who is diminished by the lady he loves. Here is a dream. Yet when the lady wakes to see her once-brave knight now a lap hound at her heels, she begins to hate what she has made. So break the leash, restore your reputation and become our dear companion once again.'

'But here is where my pleasure lies,' said Owain.

'Pleasures grow sweeter when denied,' said Gawain 'Take the path of love deferred and not the one where love burns out quickly because there is more heat than light.'

So Owain went to his lady and asked her leave to visit his old life and his old friends. 'I deserted them so suddenly in search of you.' She said that he might go, but that he must return to her within three months, and then she gave to him a ring that would protect him and be his shield.

And when the three months were coming to an end, Arthur sat one night with Owain. 'Friend, it's been a joy to have you here with us. But I know your lady misses you. When is your time to leave?'

'It's true.' Owain said. 'I should go soon. But a hunt is planned for tomorrow and I must attend.'

A few days later Arthur said, 'Owain. Is it time?'

Owain said, 'Yes. But one of the young knights I am training needs more help. I can't abandon him. Another few days should finish what's been started.'

But by the time the young knight was fully trained, the May Feast was almost upon them and who could miss that?

Then on the night of the May Feast, as all the knights sat down to supper, the great doors opened and into the hall walked the Lady of the Well. 'Here you are,' she said. 'I waited. You said you'd return but you did not. You broke your word. You have betrayed me. You killed my knight. You have displaced him, yet you do not take his place. You have defiled my well. You are nothing but a common thief. A stealer of hearts. The true knight takes his ladies heart, cherishes it and returns it to her within the time agreed. You have betrayed my love. You will not see me again.'

She stepped forward, pulled the ring from his finger and was gone.

Owain lost his love of Arthur's court
that night. Everyone had advice to give but
he did not listen or speak to anyone. He
took to wandering outside the castle gates.
One day he did not return. He had neither
king nor lady any more. He wandered as a
madman would, without purpose through
the wild, and as he went his shirt became a
greasy rag, and the hair on his body grew
thick and coarse. He lived as a creature of
the forest.

One morning a wise woman was gather-
ing herbs and roots in the dark of the forest.
She heard a snore and found him sleeping
under an oak tree. She knew nothing of him,
but felt there was something worth salvag-
ing and she brought back a horse, a sword, a
linen shirt and a pot of her best potion. She
approached the sleeping figure cautiously.
He did not wake. She took her pot of potion
and smeared it under his heart, his nose and
mouth. Then she stood beside the horse to
watch and wait.

Owain opened his eyes and sat bolt upright. He saw, with horror, what he had become. As he rose the coarse hair dropped away and he was a man again. Looking up, he saw the horse and beside it the sword. He made his way unsteadily towards them both.

The wise woman slipped the shirt over his head, helped him mount the horse and took him home, where she nursed him back to health and sanity. When he was recovered, she told him her story. She had an enemy – a knight who had stolen all her lands and wanted more besides.

Early next day, she heard Owain ride out. When she heard the sound of his returning, she opened up her door. Outside knelt her enemy. Owain held a sword above his head. The thief stuttered out, 'I'll return all your lands and more besides.'

So, leaving her better than before and restored in fortune, Owain went on his way. He was once more a knight. But where was he to go?

He rode this way and that without direction through the wilderness, and one day he heard a roar and a shriek. The noise was coming from the nearby hill. He saw there was a monstrous dragon which had a noble lion trapped against the rocks. Every time the lion tried to escape, the dragon pounced and caught it by its tail and dragged it back again. The lion was altogether overpowered by the dreadful creature. But Owain walked through the fire and with one blow brought down the fearsome beast. As he rode away, he heard a crack of twigs and a rustle of leaves behind him on the path. His horse skittered nervously. He looked back and there was the lion bounding towards him. It gave a great leap over his head and, before he could seize his sword, it had rolled over on its back in front of him. Purring, it would not let them continue until Owain had climbed from the saddle and scratched it behind the ears. Then, as he continued on his way, the lion would come alongside prancing and playing all the while as if it were a young hound he had brought up from a pup.

The evening came and they were far from any tower, so Owain made a camp. As he collected wood, the lion disappeared into the forest and soon came back with enough fuel in its jaws for three days of fire. Then the lion was off again and soon returned dragging a dead roe deer. Owain skinned the deer, put a joint onto the fire to roast and gave the rest to the lion.

Wherever Owain went, the lion was there. It would not be left behind. Whenever he came to a castle and where he was required to fight, his lion was there to protect him and nothing could contain its force.

Once he fought against a giant. The giant cried out, 'I could fight the man, but lion and man is too much.' So Owain, honourably, ordered the lion back behind the castle walls. But when the lion heard the clash of swords outside, it gave an answering roar, leapt up behind the castle gate, onto the roof of the host's hall, loped along the battlements and, jumping down, with one claw split the giant clean in two.

However hard he tried to restrain the beast, it would break out and do the killing for him. Till one day, whilst travelling through the forest, he realised he could not tell which path was which. He had been going round in circles. He and his lion were lost. Then he heard the sound of a horn and there, towering amongst the treetops, was the wild herdsman. The herdsman laughed aloud when he saw Owain and his lion. The branches of the trees thrashed as if his laughter was a storm. 'I am the one who keeps the wild wood creatures in their places. Say goodbye to your lion.' Owain stroked the lion's mane and scratched its ears one last time, and the lion bounded off to take its place beside his master.

Then the herdsman lifted his club and brought it crashing to the ground, revealing the path to the well once more. But now it was overgrown with weeds. It led him to a sad and gloomy glade of trees. All the branches were bare. There were some fallen trees that lay and rotted there. Dry leaves blew across the ground and round the old abandoned well at the centre of the glade. There was a rusty old iron pot and chain beside it. There was a stone, covered with moss. Beyond was a ruined tower.

He scraped the moss away, and sat on the stone. As he watched the clouds in the darkening day, there was another sound in the soft rattle of the dry leaves in the wind. It was a voice that echoed from the bottom of the well. 'Oh help me up. I am imprisoned here.' The iron chain was red with rust but strong enough. He threw down chain and pot and pulled the prisoner from the well. It was his lady, the lady he had kept in his heart all along.

And as they stood together, he kissed her and the clouds rolled away and showed the evening sun. She kissed him and they heard the water bubble up afresh from deep below; the wind blew all the leaves away. Then, with one more kiss, all the birds came singing to the trees.

The Lady has her knight once more.

He guards the well. The water there is sweet again. He does not stray or betray. His lion has taken up its rightful place.

At last, he has the ending he desired.

'What ending do you most desire?' asked the lady in the chapel.

'The same,' said Galahad.

'What? A beautiful lady and birds flying round your head?'

'No. To be lost and found, imprisoned and then freed again.'

'Ah! Freedom,' said the lady. 'Then you may enjoy the next tale I have to tell.'

Five

The Tale of Little Big Coat

One day a slim young lad rode into Arthur's court. His demeanor was knightly, his horse was noble, but even so, at his entrance everyone stifled a snigger. His coat, though fine, was several sizes too big for him and it was ripped and torn. He looked like a boy dressed up in his father's old coat, which is of course exactly what he was.

He walked before the King in his ill-fitting garment, bowed low to him and lower still before the Queen. He said, 'My father is dead. See where this coat is torn. That's where the weapon entered in that killed him and I will not cast his coat aside until I am worthy to wear it.'

Arthur welcomed him and told him his cause was noble and asked his name. 'Brennon the Black,' the new young lad said.

Sir Kay said, 'Rather we should call him 'Little Big Coat the Tattered' and Dagonet, who was the King's fool, let out a snort of laughter.

Arthur upbraided them both, 'Let's welcome and encourage youth, not try to shame them with cheap jokes,' but the name stuck and everyone called him 'Little Big Coat' from that day on.

Next day the King and all his knights rode out to hunt the hart and, while they were away, Queen Guinevere and her ladies and the young lads that were left behind were all picnicking on the green near the stream. Suddenly there was a roar, and a lion leapt out from the cover of the trees and ran across the meadow toward the Queen. All except Little Big Coat were afraid and fled. He did not run. He stayed. He grappled with the lion and killed it, as much by accident and enthusiasm as by skill of arms. But he had saved the Queen. So when Arthur and the knights returned and heard the tale, there was a feast for little Big Coat. Arthur made him a knight there and then.

He rose from his knees and all the men gathered round offering congratulations and slapping him on the back. And there was the venison from the hunt, well roasted, to celebrate his success. Guinevere raised her cup to him. 'Sir Brennon, we must get you a new coat.'

But he said, 'They have named me Big Coat and I will keep the name and the coat too until the time comes when I've completed my quest and gained a place of honour at Arthur's table.'

At that moment a lady entered the hall carrying a black shield, which was emblazoned with a white hand that held a white sword. She said, 'This is the shield of one who was a very noble knight. He rode out on his quest. He defeated many and was defeated in his turn. And as he lay dying, I was by his side. He gave to me this shield. It was his will and mine that I should bring it here to Arthur's court and find the young knight who is prepared to finish what that old knight began, and bring this quest of his to its end.'

'What is the quest?' asked Arthur.

'To carry this shield and meet the adventures that it brings. But you should know that to carry it comes at a cost. The price to be paid for carrying this shield is to suffer many wounds and in the end to throw it away.'

The knights looked puzzled. One of them said, 'A mysterious sort of quest.'

Another said, 'Yes. A strange sort of quest.'

Someone else asked, 'Where's the nobility in it?' Then glances were exchanged, and everyone was talking.

'What sort of a shield gets you wounds?'

'Yes! A shield should guard you from wounds.'

'Where's the aim in this quest? No aim at all.'

And Arthur said, 'Yes. It's an odd thing to take up a quest halfway through. We should ask, "Where does this quest come from? Who does it serve?"'

And that was when Big Coat stepped up. He said, 'Give me your leave to undertake this quest.'

And Arthur said, 'Oh young Sir Brennon Black! Wait for a nobler quest, fresh and more suited to your age. I wouldn't see you harmed, young as you are.'

But Big Coat was insistent. 'I will take this dead knight's uncompleted business and finish it.' So Arthur nodded and Big Coat bowed to the lady and held out his hand. She walked towards him, bowed her head and handed him the shield.

But the moment he had it in his grasp, she took a step back, looked him up and down and, with a thin smile and narrowed eyes, she turned to Arthur and said, 'His coat doesn't fit. His years are very few. He's not much good. Is this the best you have? Can you not give me one better?'

Arthur frowned at first, then smiled sadly. 'He's a good knight who has killed a lion. He needs this quest. I give him leave to go. Take our young Brennon the Black. He will grow to fit his coat.'

She asked 'Is that your name, young knight?'

'They call me Big Coat.'

'That's a better name for you. You look ridiculous. Everyone is laughing at you. You know this shield will not protect you, but rather it will mark you out. You will be the perfect target. If you take this quest, your body will be tattered as your coat is and your spirit too.'

Big Coat said, 'I understand. And now I understand too that I can expect no comfort and no soothing of my wounds from you.'

He rode out at dawn the next day on his quest and by his side rode the Lady of the Black Shield. And from the start the only words she spoke to him were harsh insults and cruel jibes.

They hadn't gone far when they heard the thunder of hooves behind them. Big Coat turned, thinking that some messenger was sending word from Arthur's court. But instead there was a rider coming fully armed towards him. The rider stopped, and called out, 'Make yourself ready to fight.' Big Coat's heart leapt with excitement. At last he was going to be put to the test. This was his first chance to fight as a knight! He raised his spear and urged his horse into a gallop to meet his opponent, and when they came together he gave a good sure blow and the strange knight hit the ground and raised the dust.

Big Coat was elated. This was easy! He seized the black shield, leapt down from his horse and with his sword in his hand cried, 'Up and meet me, man to man!' but the man on the ground made no effort to get up. Instead muffled laughter was coming from inside the helmet, and when the stranger took his helmet off, it was no knight, but Dagonet, the King's fool smirking at him from the ground.

Big Coat flushed with anger and the lady called out, 'It takes a fool to fight a fool. I daresay the only fight you'll ever win is the fight against this halfwit' and she laughed.

Dagonet's eyes and mouth widened into an expression of mock offence. 'Your lady has a sharp tongue and no mistake.' Then he laughed too. 'I bring greetings from

Sir Kay. Good luck to you, Sir Big Coat and to your Lady Sharp Tongue.' And he clambered to his feet, limped back to his horse and was away.

Big Coat and his Lady Sharp Tongue rode on, she all the while laughing heartily, 'To win against a fool. Great honour!' But he never spoke a word of reproach to her for it.

Back in King Arthur's court, Dagonet returned with the tale of his encounter. Some roared with laughter, but others were concerned about the plight of Big Coat and about his youth. Three knights agreed they would ride out to toughen him up. Two were old and experienced, Sir Bleoberis and Sir Palamedes, and they took the quick route and overtook the youth and his lady. The third was not so old nor so experienced and that was Arthur's nephew, Sir Mordred, who followed on behind.

So it was that Big Coat and his lady came at last to a meadow where the first of the old knights sat beside his horse in the shade of a tree, eating an apple. When Sir Bleoberis saw them approach, he called out, 'I recognise you lad, from Arthur's court! Come, fight me now.' He threw away the apple core, rose and climbed slowly and heavily into his saddle.

They met full tilt in the middle of the meadow, where the old knight struck him such a well-judged blow that Big Coat fell and his horse fell too. He was quickly up again, grabbing the shield and, standing firm with sword in hand, called his opponent down to fight him on foot.

But the older knight just chuckled, 'Onto your horse again youngster. Let's see how you deal with my brother in the next meadow.' He rode away.

And indeed a little further through the woods, there was the second knight, waiting on horseback. It was Sir Palamedes, one of the Muslim knights. He sat light and trim in the saddle, watching them as

they approached. He fought with a quick
deftness that brought the same result for
Big Coat. But Big Coat was not to be
defeated and was quickly up onto his own
two feet crying out a challenge, but the
only answer he got was a warm smile and
Sir Palamedes rode off without exchanging
another blow.

Big Coat took his horse and led it back
to Lady Sharp Tongue. She had one word
of comfort for him: 'Coward.' And two
questions: 'How is it that you can't seem
to stay on your horse's back long enough
to draw breath?', and, 'How is it that
the only knight that you can beat is the
King's fool?'

In reply he said, 'Please lady. I take the
blame for all my faults, but if my horse
falls to the ground, then surely I have no
choice but to go with it.' But his answer
seemed to make her more angry and her
words more wounding. As they rode on,
she continued to batter him with insults.

He never said anything, but the words cut him very deeply.

When Sir Mordred caught up with the two on the road to the infamous Castle Orgulous, he saw what a sad pair of companions they were. She was so hard-faced and angry. He was so sad and dejected. But the only wounds that Mordred could see were to the tattered coat.

Now riding to their side, he introduced himself. 'I'm Mordred, a knight of the Round Table.'

Ha!' said the lady. 'Are you another come from Arthur's court to fight and shame this little knight and knock him off his horse?'

'No. I've come to keep you company, to ride with you to the Castle Orgulous. You'll need some help there. The knights are not welcoming. They will not let us pass without a fight.'

At last they were looking down from the hill onto the castle and they were spotted at once. The gates opened and two knights rode out. Mordred smiled at Big Coat, and together they rode down to meet them on the meadow and, as they did, Big Coat felt a surge of happiness to have a friend at his side at last. Then he gave all his attention to his first blow, but was immediately on the ground again. But this time he found he'd knocked off his opponent too. He scrambled to his feet and dealt a death blow, killing the man as he had killed the lion.

He turned around in triumph, in time to see Mordred receive a mighty blow from his adversary and fall, wounded and help-less. The enemy knight turned and trotted back calmly to the gates. Big Coat ran to the horses with no riders and would have mounted on his own horse again, but Mordred cried out, 'No! You take the better – take the fresher of the three.' That was the dead knight's horse, so he jumped on that and galloped after his enemy, struck him down and slew him before he reached the gate. Then he saw that from within the castle there were many armed men, all angry, coming at him.

Outside in the meadow, the lady helped Mordred back into his saddle. They rode back onto the hill and watched the scene from there. They saw Big Coat dismount from his horse and slap its rump so that it trotted to safety. Big Coat then turned and ran with his sword waving, the black shield at his side, he ran through the castle gate. They heard the sounds of battle. A woman ran out of the postern gate, crossed the meadow, caught the reins of Big Coat's horse and led it back from whence she came, and tied it to the post there. Then they saw Big Coat come hurtling out, pursued by fighting men. He leapt onto his horse and galloped towards them. The gates were closed behind him.

Big Coat was sweating, battered, and breathless, but not wounded otherwise and wildly excited. 'Best ride on quickly,' said Mordred. 'Before the castle knights regroup and follow us in pursuit.'

As they rode, Big Coat talked loudly. 'I fought and left twelve lying there who will not be getting up again. Did you see? I killed my opponent on foot and avenged you too. I saw a host of fighting men within the walls. I was against the wall and fighting all of them. It was a lady's chamber wall. She liked my style. I heard her voice say, "Knight – you've gained much honour, killed twelve while I watched. Enough. Now slip out of the postern gate. There your horse is waiting. Ride! Don't die!" I heard her and I followed her advice. I fought with my back against the gate. Do you hear? I left twelve who will not fight again.'

Mordred was nodding and smiling, so Big Coat looked at his lady for approval. But she sneered and said, 'He's still a boy showing off to his mother, saying "Look at me!" And making up wild stories to cover his shame.'

Big Coat's shoulders sagged. But just at that moment, a messenger rode out from the Castle Orgulous. He stopped at a distance and called, 'I bring a message from my ladies. They send their greetings to the young knight who fought a noble fight. Sir, they like you! They invite you! They send you tokens of their esteem and long for you to come again so they can share their treasures with you.'

As they rode on Big Coat beamed from ear to ear, now blushing rather. And for a while the lady was silent. Until at last she said, 'It seems that even when you are not knocked off your horse, you just get off of your own accord! A strange kind of knight!'

'Lady, stop,' said Mordred. 'There's another way to look at this. It's harder to fight on horseback. All knights are easily unhorsed when young. It's easy for them to fight on foot. The young ones can do it and the older ones not so much. You'll not get an old knight getting off his horse if he can avoid it. The skill of fighting on the horse comes afterwards. We all start green. What distinguishes the lad is that he perseveres and learns. He is determined. Give this Big Coat a little credit.'

Then Mordred coughed and winced and the lady said, 'You're hurt!' They made a camp for the night and the lady tended Mordred's wounds, but ignored his words.

For many miles after that they kept company together. All the while Sir Mordred gave advice and all the while the Lady Sharp Tongue nagged.

Meanwhile at Arthur's court, Sir Lancelot had returned from travelling and at supper time heard the tale of Big Coat the Tattered and the quest of the Black Shield. He took it seriously. 'It's not good,' he said. 'It's a hard thing to take up the quest of another. It is a harder thing than to see a quest and start it and complete it on your own. I've heard of this uncompleted quest. It has defeated many. And the shield attracts as many wounds at it protects against. That this young lad should attempt it without a teacher or a mentor is shame to us all.' They told him Sir Mordred had taken on the task, but clearly he didn't think much of that and the next day he rode out too.

Riding fast and alone, he soon overtook the three of them. When Mordred saw him, Lancelot winked and Mordred knew not to speak his name. 'Now you're here, I'll return, wounded as I am,' said Mordred. He bade goodbye to the lady and her young knight, and was gone.

So now they were riding with an unknown knight and Lancelot listened while the lady continually berated Big Coat with bitter blasts.

'Mordred said you're quick to learn, but I see no sign of it,' she scolded. Big Coat said nothing, as usual. But Lancelot rebuked her for the jibe and suddenly she began a very long, loud tirade. 'If the lad can't take it, he should return home. I wish he would. His mother would say the same. And who are you to take his part anyway? You hold no shield that shows your nature nor do you tell us your name. You speak for him when you know nothing of him – who he is or what he has attempted and what he has succeeded at or failed – nor what his father was or what his father did before him and what hopes his father had for him. By what right do you protect him now?'

Everyone was rather quiet after that.

The next day Sir Lancelot said to the two, 'I have to leave you for a while. I have business nearby. Soon you'll come to the Castle Pendragon. Wait in the woods for me there and do not approach the castle till I come.'

So they rode on alone. But Big Coat found he was feeling happy; the lady's jibes didn't

seem to wound him as they had. They came
at length to the place where they were over-
looking the Castle of Pendragon. The castle
was immense and beautiful. It shone in the
sunshine. Flags fluttered from the battlements. And before it was a green meadow,
and set up there brightly coloured pavilions
and more flags fluttering, and there were
knights and horses finely clothed. Everyone
seemed to be getting ready to play and to
joust. The lady said, 'Stay here within the
cover of the wood as your friend has com-
manded.' But he rode off to get a better
look. The lady called after him, 'Our friend
has told us not to approach.' But Big Coat
wasn't listening.

Below the knights had seen him and
were calling up to him. 'Come, Sir Black
Shield. Join us in the joust!' Young Big
Coat gave a cry and rode down to the
castle. The lady shook her head, and
watched him join the others on the green.
They gave him a lance for jousting and a

fine tunic. She rode further down the slope
to get a better look and they saw her too
and called a welcome. 'Watch your young
knight joust in our friendly games.' But
she shook her head. In the first round Big
Coat rode straight and strong and was, for
the first time, the one to stay in his saddle.
It was his opponent who fell. Elated, Big
Coat turned his horse around and, taking
off his helmet, saluted the crowd. But the
other knights who watched and should
have cheered, attacked him and brought
him to the ground, dragging him dishon-
ourably through the dust before throwing
him into the castle dungeons. And the
lady was taken and imprisoned there too.
The knights, it turned out, were skilled
tricksters, robbing and imprisoning every
passing knight and lady.

When Lancelot came to the appointed
place in the wood, he found no Big Coat and
no lady, but following the horses' tracks he
came to the spot where he could see the signs

of a scuffle on the ground. He understood full well what had happened.

He saw the jousting in the meadow and was not fooled by the charade. He fell on the wily horsemen and defeated them. And when the wicked lord of the castle rode out to meet him, he defeated him too and demanded the release of Big Coat and his lady.

They opened up the gates of the prison then. But when they brought out Big Coat and the lady, blinking into the light, there issued forth behind them a crowd of one hundred lords and ladies, freed prisoners all. Lancelot cried out a commandment. 'Return to Arthur's court and take this wicked lord who has for so long tricked and imprisoned you.'

At that, they called out, 'Lancelot! Sir! Lord!'

And for the first time Big Coat and the lady realised just who it was who had accompanied them and been their friend.

Lady Sharp Tongue bowed her head before him and she spoke, 'Sir Lancelot, I call you in the name of the lady that you serve. This land and I both thank you. And, in the name of she you serve, I ask you to forgive me for my harsh tongue. My wounding words and the pain of them are the price the lad must pay for the protection of the shield.' As she spoke Big Coat, astonished, stared at her. He didn't recognise the voice, it was so soft and tender.

Lancelot said, 'Those are the sweetest words I've ever heard from your lips. We'll have to change your name.' The lady laughed and that was a sweet sound too. 'And I know that if you have learned to speak sweet, this adventure is coming to an end,' he said. They came to a river and a bridge over it that was more like a fortress, and beyond it there was a dark tower rising into the sky. There were two big knights standing guard.

'Remember,' said the Lady of the Chapel, 'when we cross over the waters, that our journey will almost be ended. While the road is the way of the knight, and the river is the way of the lady, the most blessed places are the bridges where both meet.'

The big guards of the bridge both roared out to the three companions, 'Lady! Knights! We are the ones called Force and Love. We see the black shield and will destroy anyone who tries to carry it over this bridge.'

Then the lady spoke to Big Coat. 'You've proved yourself enough my dear lad. I would not have you risk your life here.'

But Big Coat said, 'After this long road, I must try this test and win the bridge and you must let me go alone.'

He took the shield, and Lancelot and the lady let him go and fight the great knights Force and Love. And he defeated them both. In every moment, up till now, the shield had kept him free of wounds in all his fighting. But he did not have her harsh words to protect him now. This battle at the bridge, though he won it, cost him dear, and he was weak and wounded as he rode on to the tower. And when he reached it there was a strong grey grizzled old lord who said, 'I will fight you and you must know there is no lady to be won in here, but only honour.'

They fought beneath the tower and Big Coat fought well, but was cut down. The old lord defeated him. He said, 'Young knight. Were I wounded as you are I would have fallen long ago. But for your wounds, you would have defeated me and I admire you and I honour you. And though I take you prisoner now I take you in to keep you safe and heal you.' And Big Coat slept that night within the tower of the grey lord, soothed by good ointments that the lord laid on him.

When the morning came Big Coat heard voices from below and, looking out, saw Lancelot and the lady calling up to the lord. 'Come down. You have a friend of ours imprisoned there. You cannot keep him any more.'

His captor stood beside him at the window. 'You have won yourself the very best of friends. And as I know the knight I go to fight is Lancelot, you can be sure you'll soon be free and then it's you who will be lord of this tower.'

The battle between the lord and Lancelot wasn't long. The great knight spared the life of the lesser. The lady helped Big Coat from the tower, and Lancelot said, 'Now, Big Coat. Take this tower that is your own.'

But Big Coat said, 'I can't. This lord has cared for me and given me back my life. How can I cast him from his tower? My quest till now has been unclear and hidden in mystery. But now I'm here and it's complete, I see it's possible to take what's needed and leave the rest behind.'

And then he took off his father's tattered black coat and wrapped it round the black shield, and he went to the bridge and dropped both shield and coat into the dark waters. He watched the bubbles rise and the ripples spread and, when the water was still again, they all went home to Arthur's court. The grey lord went with them and all three knights were welcomed there and given seats at the Round Table where they belonged.

By now you know that none of these knights were the ones to take up the special place – neither brave Sir Lancelot nor Mordred ever sat in the the perilous seat. Neither did Big Coat. He was not the best, but he had the best of friends and was the best that he could be.

And as for Lady Sharp Tongue, she became Lady Sweet Tongue, saying, 'I was the price. Now I will be the prize.' And as the last of the hard lines of judgement softened from her face, Big Coat saw the beauty that she'd hidden since the day he took the shield from her. They married and at the wedding, he wore a new coat that fitted him perfectly.

Now, when he's not at Camelot, he stands guard with his own shield and his own sword and his sons stand with him and his Lady Sweet Tongue says, 'Just look at them! Each one is as handsome, kind and noble as his father.'

They guard the Castle of Pendragon and ensure that none will be imprisoned there ever again.

The lady sat in the shadows of the chapel. Galahad stared into the candle flame.

'Of all the knights who spoke in praise of the Queen at the May Festival, no one spoke the words more fervently and no one felt the words more deeply than did Sir Lancelot of the Lake. And it was his

adventure, his quest that was to change the nature and the power of Guinevere and of the ladies of the lake forever. He did not ask for his great quest or enjoy the adventure. But he accepted it.'

Six

The Queen of the Wasteland

This is your father's story and your mother's story and the story of your birth.

Lancelot was riding out on the road one day when he saw a bridge in the distance. There was a group of farmers, stewards and washerwomen standing beside it, and one man saw him approach, broke away and ran towards him. 'Sir!

Cross our Bridge of Corbin. Come and save us all. We need a good knight, one who is fearless and bold. Someone like you!'

'Tell me what kind of help you need,' said Lancelot.

'We have a lady, daughter of our good King. Her name is Elaine and she is under a spell, an enchantment. She's been trapped in a steaming chamber these last five years.'

'Well, if I can help, I will,' said Lancelot.

Soon they reached the bridge, which stood unguarded by any knight, and the man took Lancelot's horse and led him over. The people crowded round. They greeted him and walked beside the horse. He saw that the fields in the land were dry, wild and unkempt. The crops were choked with weeds and the leaves of the apple trees were blistered with a canker. As he rode he listened to the stories of the folk who followed him. 'Poor young lady! She started so well – a beautiful and promising child. Always playing by the river! But as she grew in power and beauty, it seemed something went wrong. Anyhow, all we know is as she stews in there, something terrible is happening to the rivers and the streams of our land.'

'Who knows what it was that went wrong. Some say she attracted the attention and the anger of the Great Queens of Morgan.'

'No, I think it's the father who's to blame.'

'Sh! Don't say that! He's our King. Anyway how is he responsible for the wound that will not heal?'

'Perhaps not to blame, but it's strange that once he got that wound the land began to wither, and the next thing we know it's the girl that's suffering.'

'Well, whatever it was, the power that looked so promising when it was young and unformed that we thought would make our river run sweeter and clearer, has instead dried it up.'

'One day she went to bathe at our forest pool, but as she entered, the water began to bubble and boil, and when she tried to leave the water, she could not.'

They had reached a place where a tower stood on a rocky hillside. Lancelot shaded his eyes against the sun and looked up. Though the day was clear, the tower was hidden in mist and cloud. 'We built this tower to contain her pain. There she sits, imprisoned day and night under some curse, that's for sure. It keeps her stuck and we hear her cry out in the night, "My body burns!", "Who was it lit this fire?", "Am I to be boiled to nothing?" Others have tried to free her, but none can face the torrid heat. It's a place of scalding, sweltering fever. We know that only the best of knights can save her and be the means of releasing her from the place where she cooks.'

Lancelot looked up at the tower. 'I've never met this sort of quest before. If I try and fail, then it will only be the same for her but worse, leaving her sadder and more tortured than before.'

But how could he ride away and leave her? He left his horse entrusted to the gate-keeper. As he approached he saw that there was an open entrance to the tower, and when he looked back, the man nodded to him encouragingly.

Within there were steps spiraling upwards, but as he put his foot on the first one, he heard the gatekeeper call, 'Not up sir! Down! Go down. She's down.' And, sure enough, there was a corresponding set of steps disappearing down into the dark-ness. They were well worn.

He was descending into a cloud of steam that billowed into his face and stung his hands and cheeks. He closed his eyes against the heat and vapour. He heard from deep below a gurgle and a bubbling. He was wet with sweat and his mailed feet slipped on the rock. There was a strange sweet scent that made him dizzy and light-headed. There was a strange light, too. He peered through the steam and realised he had come to a chamber where water dripped from the ceiling.

He thought he saw a woman. She seemed to be within the bubbling ferment of the water and in her hands she held a bowl. He staggered.

It seemed for one moment that she was very far away and small and was herself within the bowl. Then suddenly she was very close indeed, naked and thin as a needle, and the bowl like a golden coracle around her. On her face there was such a look of loss and hopelessness that he could not help but reach out to her, naked as she was.

But his hands closed around a metal chain. He thought, 'A golden chain binds her to the bowl!' And behind the bubbling of the water he heard her muttering all the while, 'Will we all be cooked and broiled and boiled and stewed until the goodness has gone out of us? Where will we find the little stream? Who will conjure the river? Who will encourage the rains?' He pulled on the chain and it scalded and blistered him. But even so he kept on pulling it and with it pulled her to the step. He reached for her and, as he touched her, the bubbling of the boiling water seemed to turn to geysers and spurt up in steamy fountains. He pulled her from the steam. Her skin was mottled red, and wet, and for a moment she felt so hot and rigid that he thought it was the bowl itself he held in his hands. He lifted her and carried her clear and up the steps. His head cleared. It was a woman he held. It was soft skin he felt.

Some of the servants from the bridge were waiting in the sunlight in the company of a well-dressed dame. She was short and plump and course-faced. 'Quick, girls, linen!' she snapped.

Two bobbed and chorused, 'Yes Dame Brisen,' and they returned with towels, blankets and a shift. They wrapped their lady in the blankets as Dame Brisen said, 'Come, dear child. Elaine! I'll mix a potion and make enchantments that will heal you. A little of my magic will soon have you right as rain.' Dame Brisen put out her arm, but the young woman pulled away from her and turned and looked at him. He saw how pale she was in the sunlight and how very lovely.

She said, 'I must get dry. Then, sir, we must go to the chapel to pray to God.' That was a surprise. She looked tired and sad, not at all like a woman who had been saved from evil magic and rescued and returned to life and is glad of it.

But the people were round him cheering and shouting, and then some were calling for the King. A thin old man swathed in blankets was carried through the crowd. Elaine went to him and took his hand.

The old King turned to Lancelot and said, 'A deed is done today. My daughter is restored to us. Thank you, Sir Knight, for saving her from the magic and the influence of the dread queens.' Then he fell back into the arms of his attendants and was carried away.

That evening the King held a feast and when the meat, the honey cakes, the beer and the mead were all laid out, Elaine entered, dressed in cloth of grey and black. In her hands she carried a shining cup and gave it to Lancelot. As he drank, he thought for a moment that the steam from the boiling pool was again upon his face and he felt the metal was hot in his hands. But then it was cool again and he realised the blistered fingers that had pained him and throbbed all through the day were now healed. The King saw his uncertainty and said, 'This is the power of the grail! And you are the knight who will mend what's shattered and lead us out of this wasteland. My daughter is to be the mother of the greatest knight of all – one who will restore us all to what is lost. And you are destined to be father of that wondrous child.'

Lancelot shook his head. 'You are mistaken. This can't be.'

'And yet this child must come to be,' said the King. 'The Round Table has had its day. It will crack and come apart. The future lies with us.'

'No,' said Lancelot. 'It was chance that brought me here today and I was glad to help. But I must return to Camelot and my lady. My honour and my loyalty belong to Guinevere, the Queen of mysteries. I cannot marry.'

The old King glanced at Elaine, and at Dame Brisen standing by. He shrugged and said, 'Ah well. He will have none but his Lady Guinevere.'

The Dame exchanged a look with him. 'Let me deal,' she said, and left the hall.

That night Dame Brisen took herbs picked at dawn and roots gathered by moonlight, and took pestle and mortar, pounded a potion and made the magic that she needed. She drugged his bedtime drink and placed an enchantment of disguise upon herself.

Later that night a knock came to Lancelot's door. Looking out, he saw a soldier dressed in the manner of Arthur's court, but rather short and plump.

Lancelot asked, 'Do you come from the Queen?'

'I do.'

'Is she nearby?'

'She is.'

'Does she want me by her?'

'She does.'

Quickly Lancelot was into his clothes and tying his straps and his laces and was out of the door and along the corridor, following the short plump soldier to horse and then over the hill. There was a castle and Lancelot followed the soldier to a door.

'Is this the Queen's chamber?' Lancelot asked.

'Sir, open the door.' So he did.

'But it's so dark,' said Lancelot. 'I cannot see my way at all.'

'Then let me guide you,' said a soft voice. And a soft hand took his.

'Take off your clothes,' said the voice.

'But I cannot see the straps at all.'

'Then let me help you,' and sure hands undressed him.

'But I cannot see my Queen at all.'

'Then let me take you to her.'

Now he lay under silken covers and a soft hand touched his chest and a soft thigh covered his and soft lips kissed his own. And Dame Brisen left the room and shut the door gently behind her.

The morning sun dissolved the magic. Something was stirring in the room. Lancelot opened his eyes. It was Elaine who was coming to his bedside smiling, with a morning cup. He asked, 'Where's my Queen, Guinevere?'

Elaine looked within the cup. 'Guinevere is not here, and never was here.' Then she looked directly at him and said, 'I am the only queen here.'

Then he knew he had been tricked and horror and fury overwhelmed him. He was a man of action at his heart. He leapt to his feet, pulled his sword from the sheath and roared, 'Queen of deception! Is this how you repay me?'

In his fury he would have wielded the sword and taken off her head, had she not thrown herself at his feet and cried, 'Yes. True. You are deceived. I am not she. I have fulfilled my own desire and the wishes of my father. But it's also true that I love you and that I now have within me the beginnings of a most extraordinary child. There's no deception there and that cannot be changed. Don't kill me. Stay here with me and with your son.'

He was ashamed of himself, now, to be standing naked over the woman with the sword in his hand. He let it fall. He lifted her up and kissed her gently on the forehead. But he would not stay, and later that day he returned to Arthur's court.

And when her time came, Elaine gave birth to her little son, with Dame Brisen, the always-resourceful midwife, in attendance. He was a shining baby; good tempered and happy and, as he grew, a quiet, wise child who never seemed to miss the guidance of a father. She named him Galahad.

Then, one day news came that there would be a festival at Camelot. Elaine went to her father, the King, 'Let me go and visit Arthur's court.'

'Well if you must then go. But go dressed as the most high and bright of queens. Let your high state be seen by all.'

The night before the festival, Sir Lancelot was alone in his chamber, when his lady, Queen Guinevere, came to him.

'Lancelot. Another queen has arrived. Elaine is here.'

'Elaine is not a queen,' he replied.

'She is dressed in silks and satins.'

'Silks and satins do not make a queen.'

'She comes with fifty ladies and with fifty soldiers all on horseback.'

'Ladies and soldiers do not make a queen.'

'She comes with a little child. He has your eyes, Lancelot. It seems that a bridge has been crossed. It seems that times are changing. It seems my power is waning.'

'No. Nothing has changed!' he said.

When Arthur and his Queen greeted Elaine, Lancelot stood by Guinevere's side. Arthur's welcome was warm and courteous. Guinevere's smile was hospitable. But when Elaine looked at Lancelot, she saw only shame upon his face.

Lancelot was remembering not that he had been tricked; but that he had stood over her with a sword and would have cut her head off, and that he had betrayed his lady, the Queen.

Later, in her chamber, as Dame Brisen brushed down her hair, Elaine said, 'What shall I do? For five years I have thought of him, his touch, his look, his kiss. Now he won't even look at me.'

Dame Brisen said, 'Let me deal.'

That night, when Lancelot answered the knock at his chamber door, he saw a short plump soldier. He struggled to remember where he had seen this soldier before, but magic muddles the clearest minds and again he followed Dame Brisen into the darkness.

This time, it was a different light that woke him. He opened his eyes calling out the name 'Guinevere'. And there was the Queen herself. She stood at the door. Her radiance had banished the darkness, and all too late the magic as well. He saw the face on the pillow next to his – the face of Elaine, and he leapt from the bed and in his undershirt stood uncertain between the lady in the bed and the lady at the door. Then he turned his back on both, opened up the chamber window and jumped into the garden before running half naked through the thorn trees. Then he was gone.

In the chapel, Galahad shook his head. The lady of the chapel nodded and said, 'Your father was unbeatable and indisputably the best knight of his time, but his power was always ambiguous and mysterious. He could never untangle this knot.'

Lancelot ran wild for many months. His shirt became a greasy rag, his body was neglected, wasted, besmeared and scarred. His hair and beard were tangled, matted with mud and snagged by burrs. He lived off berries and roots. He went running wildwood with the animals deep into the darkness of the forest. He might have run deeper still, his mind more confused than it had been under the magic of Dame Brisen, more clouded than by the vapours of the boiling pool. But one day, he wandered into a clearing.

There was a pavilion, scarlet penants flapping in the breeze. On an oak tree hung a shield, two swords and a spear. He was drawn to the weapons. He grasped a sword and with it he beat and beat with a frenzied clamour on the shield.

Out ran a servant to reclaim his master's sword, but a blow from the back of Lancelot's hand sent him flying flat on his back. The noise brought out the knight himself, his shirt flapping loose. He reached to wrest the sword from Lancelot's grip, but a quick left hook sent him reeling across the ground.

Then Lancelot dropped the sword and staggered into the pavilion. He collapsed onto the bed and fell asleep beside the lady who was resting there. She leapt up and ran to join her knight and servant outside, and helped them to their feet and back into the pavilion. The knight said, 'This madman packs a punch.'

But the servant said, 'Sir, I've seen him before. I saw him joust in France.'

'Joust? In France?'

'Yes. This is a knight in great trouble.' The knight and lady now looked with understanding at the figure on the bed.

When they returned to their home on the far edge of the forest, they carried with them the still sleeping Lancelot. They fed him, cared for him and tried to tame the wildness in him, but could not restore the madman to his wits. At last he wandered off along the margins of the woods until he found an empty shack outside a castle wall, and there he would sleep and roam subject to the kindness and cruelty of strangers. Sometimes there was a blow for him. He returned that threefold.

Sometimes there was a blessing or a smile
for him. He returned that with a look of
blank bewilderment.

One day, the local lord held a feast.
He was giving gifts to everyone. 'Bring in
the madman,' he said. 'We'll have a little
sport.' When Lancelot came shuffling
into the hall, the servants brought out a
fine red cloak and put it on his shoulders.
'Now you're the lord,' he said, and took
him to the seat of honour. Everyone roared
with laughter. But when he sat down in the
seat and looked around, all laughter died
away. He had such dignity and presence.
And when he rose and stepped down from
the throne, the crowd of people parted
before him and some found they couldn't
help but bow. They watched him walk
from the hall, into the garden and out to
the orchard beyond.

The next morning a golden-haired boy
was running through the apple trees,
picking up the windfalls as he went. But

when the boy returned to his mother he was quite solemn and took her soft pale hand in his little one. He led her to a place beneath an old apple tree where a man in a red cloak lay sleeping, and for all his beard and tangled hair she knew him at once. They took him to a cloud-topped tower. They carried him not down the steps, but up, into a room where Dame Brisen dealt one last time. There Elaine gave him the sacred cup. He opened his eyes. He saw her, smiled a sad smile and asked, 'Where am I?'

'Where are you? You are home,' she said

She said, 'Do you not know me?'

He didn't know her.

She kissed him on the forehead and said: 'I lost you in a garden of thorns.I found you in a garden of flowers.And all the time that you were lost, the pain I felt when I lay in the boiling pool was nothing to pain I felt at the loss of you and the joy I felt at the touch of your cool hand was nothing to the joy I feel at the sight of you now. You were mad, but now you're sane and you are home. You are in the grail castle where you belong, with the ones who love you.'

He knew her then. 'My mind and my body are restored and I thank you. But I am not home and I can never be home. Ask your father in his grace for a place for me and promise me you'll never speak of what has passed.'

He stayed. He had nowhere else to go. She stayed beside him.

But at last the news came that the Queen forgave him, had never really blamed him. When he heard that, he left for good, that very day, and Elaine never saw him again.

'It is almost at an end,' said the lady of the chapel. Galahad stared into the candle as it struggled to hold its flame. The shapes and figures of the tales were all dying with the light. 'Your father always knew the seat could never be his. He was always in Camelot because his lady was there, but he

was never truly in Camelot, because she was the Queen and he could never be her lord there. In the end, the greatest knight in the world was just a man – but what a man!' she said with a smile.

'You know the rest,' she said. 'The sword in the stone that hovered over the water, the empty seat you took, the vow you made.'

'Yes,' he said, 'and now we must continue on a journey not of words, but of deeds.'

'You are right,' she said. 'That's enough looking back. The future calls us now.'

She extinguished the light and as the sun was rising led Galahad out of the chapel. They mounted their horses and rode side by side. Now they were on the move, she was a young girl once more.

Lower down in the valley, another knight was following the river to its source. He came to the stone chapel. He looked in through the little window, but for him the light had been put out and within was only darkness. The door was barred. He pounded, but no lady came to open it. So Sir Lancelot turned away and rode alone back to Arthur's court.

Galahad and the lady of the chapel rode on to the sea shore, where two familiar figures, Sir Percival and Sir Bors, stood waiting. Percival rushed to greet the lady.

'You know her?' asked Galahad.

'Of course! She is my sister,' said Sir Percival.

'Well, she has been a mother to me,' said Galahad.

'Mother?' cried Sir Bors.

'She changes in the light,' said Galahad, with a smile.

'Damn the light,' said Sir Bors, 'Sister to one! Mother to the other! How about wife to me?' And he smiled hopefully.

But the lady walked away from them towards the waves where a boat was waiting to carry them across the waters.

As soon as they began to sail, the lady

asked Galahad for his sword. She took it and cut off her long hair. Then she took the hair and, with strips of gold and silk, began to weave. As she wove she told a tale:

Once there was a garden and in the garden there stood the first apple tree. A lady sheltered beneath its branches. The lady lived in the garden but she was forbidden to eat the fruit from that tree. But one day she was hungry and the tree took pity on her and bent down its branches so that she might eat. She reached up but when she touched the branch, it turned white and then the sky went dark. Lightning struck the tree and the bough broke and fell to the ground. She picked it up and, as the storm raged around her, she ran with it from the garden and kept on running until she came to a wasteland. She planted the bough in the earth and began to sing and, as she sang, the bough grew into a great, white apple tree. She sat beneath it and kept on singing. A man heard her and he followed the sound through forests, deserts and across oceans, until he came to the place where she was. She stopped singing. She liked him and he liked her and they both liked the apple tree. So they lay beneath it and there the first child was born into the world as the tree blossomed above them.

As they were sailing on the waters, the lady continued to tell her tale. She wove the patterns of their lives into the thing that she was making. She told the story of their world from its beginning through to that moment when they all stepped ashore onto the other side.

There she took the thing that she had made and gave it to Galahad, saying, 'This is a new girdle for a new age.' And she tied it around his waist and said, 'Now Balin's sword has found its resting place.'

As the sun beat down, they walked on across parched earth. At last they came to a boiling pool, and around it sat women, men and children, each one no more than a bag of bones. Thin and hollowed eyed, the people stared at them in silence. Then one young girl looked up at Galahad and said, 'Sir, please help us. This water cannot quench our thirst.'

Galahad went to the edge of the pool and raised his arms into the air. 'In the name of my father. In the name of my mother.' Then he plunged his hands into the boiling waters. And the pool cooled and the people could drink again.

The four companions travelled until they came to the gates of a castle, half ruined, yet still mighty.

The guards would not let them enter. 'There is a rule of entry. Within, our Queen suffers and is sick. Your company cannot pass through our gates unless your lady gives up her blood. We need a basinful. The blood will be the medicine to heal our Queen.'

'No,' said Galahad. 'This lady can't be harmed. Yet we will still come in.' All three guards raised their swords and a battle raged there at the gates of Corbin Castle. But no one could best Balin's blade when held in Galahad's hand.

Soon the three guards lay defeated and humbled at his feet, and Percival and Bors went to open wide the gates.

But the lady stopped them and spoke gently to the guards. 'Bring out your Queen to me.'

The guards carried out their Queen, pale and weak, and gently laid her on the ground in front of them.

A silver basin was brought. 'Please sister,' pleaded Percival. 'Don't do this.'

'I give what is needed freely so that no other woman need suffer in this way again.'

And as she gave of herself, she became pale and weak.

'Stop. That's enough,' cried Sir Bors.

'Do not be afraid,' she said. 'I am the

cup that overflows, that fills the pools and the lakes with the waters that ebb and flow across land.' And with that the life of the lady was gone and the Queen of the Wasteland made whole again.

The three knights carried their lady's body to the sea shore. Then they set her upon the waters to float again amongst the stars.

Then they returned to the Grail Castle and entered the great hall. There in the darkness was the Queen restored. In her arms she cradled an ancient wasted man with a golden crown upon his head, by his side a shining spear.

Galahad knelt down, took the old King's hand in his and whispered, 'Grandfather, what ails thee?'

Then he took the spear with which Balin had wounded the King. He held it balanced in his hands. 'Great King, know that what harms can also heal.' He placed the point of the spear against the flow from the wound and the King was healed and the wasteland restored.

It took many months for all the knights to return to Camelot; all that would return, that is. And most had not achieved what they had set out for. Then it came to Pentecost again, at Arthur's court. It was the feast of tongues, but now no one spoke. Galahad sat in his rightful place at the Round Table. He looked around at the faces of all the other men gathered there and saw the marks that told the tales of the hardships that they had endured. Many chairs were empty now.

The King signalled for the most worthy of knights to speak. 'This table,' said Galahad, 'is a mighty mirror whose curves reflect the roundness of the world. You, its company of knights, are like the spheres orbiting the earth. Your King, our sun, a fixed point in the firmament around which the whole universe can dance. Surrender your hearts and your ears to me now, for

words can come to the head like a whis-
tling wind which blows about and is gone
again. Your hearts must hold onto what
I have to say if my true meaning is to be
known. Stand under my words now and
take shelter in them. I will not speak of
dreams or fables as others have. I will
simply tell you what I have seen.'

And as Galahad recounted his journey,
his words fell like flakes of snow into the
heart of the hall, and, when there were no
more words, in that great white silence each
knight heard what he was hungry for.

The one who felt defeated in spirit heard
'hope'.

The one who felt murder in his soul
heard 'mercy'.

The one who felt dead in his body heard
'live'.

The one who felt the tragedy of his time
heard the joke and began to laugh and laugh.
Then as all the knights laughed together,
the doors of the hall opened and in walked

the Queen of the Wasteland carrying a golden crown.

She bowed towards King Arthur. Galahad rose from the Seat Perilous and knelt before his mother. Then, holding that circle of gold above his head, she said, 'What was broken is mended. What was wounded is healed. My father's time is passed. I bring his crown. It's yours my son. Be a new king for a new age.'

Then that great Queen and her two Kings led the knights out into the light and all around them the land burst back into life.

Further Reading/ Bibliography/Sources

Elizabeth Archibald and A.S.G. Edwards,
    A Companion to Malory
Sioned Davies, *The Mabinogion*
Sir Thomas Malory, *The Morte D'Arthur*
Wolfram Von Eschenback, *Parzival*
Alan Lupack, *Oxford Guide to Arthurian
    Literature and Legend*
P.M. Matarasso, *The Quest of the Holy Grail*
Caitlin and John Matthews, *Ladies of the Lake*

Patricia Parkes, *Inescapable Romance*

Felicity Riddy, *Sir Thomas Malory*

Chretien de Troyes, *Arthurian Romances*

Jessie L. Weston, *Lais of Marie de France and Others*

Anne Wilson, *The Magical Quest: The Use of magic in Arthurian Romance*

Anne Wilson, *Plots and Powers: Magical Structures in Medieval Narrative*

If you enjoyed this book, you may also be interested in …

Denbighshire Folk Tales

FIONA COLLINS

Fiona Collins has collected a wide range of tales here. People unfamiliar with the culture and customs of the county will find some fascinating and unusual tales. Denbighshire has inspired stories of magic, dragons and devils and ordinary people doing extraordinary things.

978 0 7524 5187 9

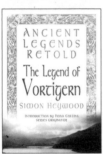

Ancient Legends Retold: The Legend of Vortigern

SIMON HEYWOOD

Generations before Arthur's birth, a British warlord looks back on his life. Vortigern's voice speaks from the heart of a forgotten darkness, telling a story of courage and cowardice, glory and crime, tragedy and treason.

978 0 7524 9004 5

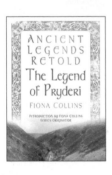

Ancient Legends Retold: The Legend of Pryderi

FIONA COLLINS

Pryderi is a figure from the earliest days of Welsh legend. The stories tell of a great warrior; a hero of the battlefield, who inhabited a world of magic and might. In this book, his legend is retold for a new generation.

978 0 7524 9005 2

Visit our website and discover thousands of other History Press books.

www.thehistorypress.co.uk

The History Press